ALL RIGHT
Original Works Publishing

CAUTION: Professionals and amateurs are hereby warned that this play is subject to royalty. It is fully protected by Original Works Publishing, and the copyright laws of the United States. All rights, including professional, amateur, motion pictures, recitation, lecturing, public reading, radio broadcasting, television, and the rights of translation into foreign languages are strictly reserved.

The performance rights to this play are controlled by Original Works Publishing and royalty arrangements and licenses must be secured well in advance of presentation. PLEASE NOTE that amateur royalty fees are set upon application in accordance with your producing circumstances. When applying for a royalty quotation and license please give us the number of performances intended, dates of production, your seating capacity and admission fee. Royalties are payable with negotiation from Original Works Publishing.

Royalty of the required amount must be paid whether the play is presented for charity or gain and whether or not admission is charged. Particular emphasis is laid on the question of amateur or professional readings, permission and terms for which must be secured from Original Works Publishing through direct contact.

Copying from this book in whole or in part is strictly forbidden by law, and the right of performance is not transferable.

Whenever the play is produced the following notice must appear on all programs, printing, and advertising for the play:
"Produced by special arrangement with
Original Works Publishing.
www.originalworksonline.com"

Due authorship credit must be given on all programs, printing and advertising for the play.

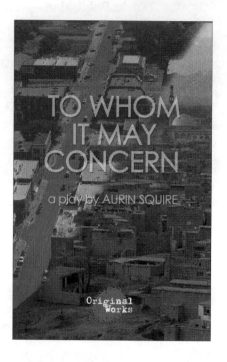

Synopsis: *To Whom It May Concern* is an epistolary play about transcendent and oft-kilter ways of love and internet relationships. When a 15- year-old boy writes a letter to a soldier and is confused for an older woman, a series of seductive exchanges begins, leading to an explosive encounter.

Cast Size: 2 Males

Defacing Michael Jackson

By
Aurin Squire

Defacing Michael Jackson was first produced by Flying Elephant Productions in Chicago, IL on July 27, 2018. The production was directed by Alexis J. Roston and the cast and crew was as follows:

Cast (in alphabetical order):
JACK - Samuel Martin
FRENCHY - Jory (JoJo) Pender
RED, YELLOW, COMMISH - Eldridge Shannon
OBADIAH - Christopher Taylor

Production Team:
Nicholas Schwartz (scenic design)
Petter Wahlbäck (sound design)
Jesse Gowens (costume design)
Becs Bartle (lighting design)
Jordan Affeldt (stage manager)

SETTING

1984. The arid and abandoned land of Opa Locka, Florida.

CHARACTER BREAKDOWN

The story is told with four actors.

FLORIDA TRACK A:
1. OBADIAH – light-skin teenage black boy and older adult man who narrates.

FLORIDA TRACK B:
1. FRENCHY– dark-skinned black teenager

FLORIDA TRACK C:
1. RED– mentally-challenged black twin
2. YELLOW - other black twin who stutters
3. CITY COMMISSIONER - black commissioner

FLORIDA TRACK D:
1. JACK – white teenage boy new to area.

DIRECTOR'S NOTES

The stage is bare for almost the entire play. The objects in the play can be mimed, but it's the directors choice as to how many objects. The actors should be specific with objects mimed.

Obadiah narrates the story as an older man, but lives in the piece as a teenager. Light shifts reflect a change from present to past as well as a jump to a new locations. The scene changes are minimal and the entire play should flow together without stopping.

The MJ mural can be mimed as well. If it exists then it can be created through slides, video, or just fragments of photos. As long as there is a sense of regeneration and disintegration throughout the play.

DEFACING MICHAEL JACKSON

ACT ONE

SCENE ONE

OBADIAH: Can you take yourself back? Before the rub-
ble and ash of the Twin Towers, Oklahoma City and
Waco. Before crack, Columbine, Atkins, and AIDS.
Further back, before Clarence and Anita, Bush and
Quayle, Jim and Tammy Faye, even further! Before
televangelists, telemarketing and *Teletubbies*. And here
we are. The year of the eternal future: 1984. Opa
Locka, Florida: a flat city of gasoline stations, abandoned parking lots, and a drainage canal where every
year a few drunks drown in the weed-choked black water that carry waste from Miami and into the Ever-
glades. A place where something is always getting
started and nothing is ever finished. This is the edge. Of
black and white. Of innocence and corruption. Of naïve
optimism and jaded cynicism. Of the fading cold war
and the approaching hot peace. Metal jacks and *Thun-
dercats*. *GI Joes* and *Cabbage Patch*. And rising above
it all is one man who they come to see. I aesthetically
structured the room so that all eyes could see. They
filed in with rubber bands, cracker jack toys and sticky
sweet and sour fingers. The lights are turned off 30 sec-
onds before the beginning. To set the mood. And the
crowd hushes in reverential silence. Can you go back? I
can.

*(LIGHTS SHIFT. OBADIAH is a teenager shouting at his
friends.)*

OBADIAH: All right! Hey, quiet! My parents are in the
other room. No fighting, no talking, and definitely no
eating candy or food. My mom would kill me. We've
only got a sofa and a loveseat and it has to last. We got
Lays and Ritz, and that's all you getz. If you've already

7

seen him once this week, go to the back, greedy. Relax, you're in my home. My living room. My family. And if any of you have seen the retarded twins down the block, tell them to give me back my bike.

SCENE TWO

(FRENCHY, a sassy, dark-skinned teenager settles down a group of kids. Red, a mean-snarky teen, stands beside her.)

FRENCHY: A-ight, let's get started. I said let's get started y'all. Simmer down. BOY, YOU BETTA SIMMER DOWN! *(over-official sounding)* Welcome to 'The Opa Locka City and Miami-Dade County, Florida Michael Jackson Fan Club.' As your president, Yvonne "Frenchy" Carter, I call this meeting to order. Now let's get down to business because I got great news and I ain't tryin' to mess around w'ich y'all today. The first thing you can do is thank me because I am the best president ever.

RED: You da only president ever.

FRENCHY: I'm the only one qualified to fill the shoes of being responsible enough to do this, Red.

RED: You da' HNIC. For now.

FRENCHY: Thanks for the fortune cookie, Niggadamus.

OBADIAH: -Frenchy! Get to the news.

FRENCHY: Well ANY-way. The city of Opa Locka is finally starting to come around to our love of Michael Jackson: the greatest musician and entertainer in the whole universe. I mean, did you see what he did on-

OBADIAH: -Frenchy.

FRENCHY: Ahem. As I was saying Opa Locka wants to honor Michael Jackson and wants us teens -and even retarded kids like Red- to be involved. So they're gonna build a giant mural on the city hall building wall!

9

And we're going to get to help make a monument to Michael. I'm telling you this is just the sort of thing that'll bring the Jacksons in to town. Get a mural, a few statues, maybe a theme park.

OBADIAH: We can just start with the mural first. This is kind of exciting. A mural. Wow.

(BEAT)

OBADIAH: What is a mural?

FRENCHY: It's a thing, okay. A very big thing. So stop bothering me about dumb details. A mural is a fancy work of art. And it's gonna have Michael Jackson on it.

RED: Better keep Frenchy's face away from it or she'll crack the whole damn picture.

FRENCHY: *(fake laughing)* Ahahahaha...that's so funny Red. No wonder you and your brother came out retarded. Your momma probably saw your face and tried to shove you back in.

OBADIAH: How are we gonna do this mural thing?

FRENCHY: Well, I, as your trusted president have been put in charge of it. I'm gonna be picking out different fans to help put it together. Don't worry, Obie you're at the top of my list.

OBADIAH: You'd do that for me?

FRENCHY: Hold me.

OBADIAH: What?

FRENCHY: I mean... I'd do anything for my favorite Michael Jackson fan club treasurer. Any other news?

RED: *(breaking their intimacy)* There's a new family that moved in down the street!

FRENCHY: You bug-eyed muthafucka-

OBADIAH: -Frenchy!

FRENCHY: *(composing herself)* Ahem. Okay? So you think we should invite them into the club?

RED: No, we should see if they got any cool stuff we can sneak on.

FRENCHY: Meeting adjourned.

(Lights shift.)

OBADIAH: As it turns out the mural would be a pretty big deal. It would be a collection of Michael Jackson memorabilia from fans. We would all get a chance to have our voices heard.

SCENE THREE

(YELLOW and FRENCHY play jacks. Yellow, the light-skinned twin of Red, is a boy with a speech impediment. After a toss, he swipes some of the jacks.)

FRENCHY: Uh-uh! Gimme back my jacks.

YELLOW: I w-w-win.

FRENCHY: You cheatin'!

YELLOW: Fu-fu-fair as square.

FRENCHY: Youze a lying cheatin' retard.

YELLOW: ...ah-ah-I nu-never lie.

FRENCHY: I'm finna go to Obie's house becuz I ain't playin' wit you no more. Gimme back my jacks, retard!

YELLOW: Nu-nuh-uh, ugly!

FRENCHY: Who you calling ugly, retard! You so stupid that when you count to ten, you get stuck at one.

YELLOW: Your...so ugly w-when you t-take a bath the water j-jumps out.

FRENCHY: Yeah, well you're so stupid that you took a blood test and failed.

YELLOW: Yuh-you so ugly you make onions cry.

FRENCHY: That ain't nuthin' because you so stupid that you tried to mail a letter with food stamps. You so stupid, you took a ruler to bed to see how long you slept! You is so stupid! That, that...they had to burn down the second grade to get your ass out of it. That's how stupid you are!

YELLOW: So? My momma said you uglier than s-s-sin on Sunday. Yuh-yuh-you so ugly... your doctor is a vet. Wuh-when you g-get up, th-the s-sun goes down. Yuh-you s-so ugly that if-f ugly wuh-were br-bricks you'd be the Guh-Great Wall of Ch-China. D-d-damn...youze ugly!

FRENCHY: Gimme back my jacks!

YELLOW: Muh-make me!

FRENCHY: Ima tell yo moma!

YELLOW: S-so? M-my momma don't like you. S-she said you t-too ugly.

FRENCHY: Then Imma tell my moma!

(YELLOW drops the jacks and FRENCHY scoops them up. She begins to leave.)

YELLOW: Wait!

FRENCHY: What? *(imitating)* 'Yuh-yuh-you g-g-got s-something t-to s-say?'

YELLOW: A secret.

FRENCHY: No you don't?

YELLOW: Uh-huh.

FRENCHY: Nobody else knows? *(He shakes his head 'no'.)* Why not?

YELLOW: S-s-savin it.

FRENCHY: 'Chamon, Yellow. Tell me, fool!

YELLOW: *(wags finger)* Fuh-fuh-first, the rest of the jacks.

FRENCHY: You are evil.

(FRENCHY hands over the rest of the jacks to Yellow.)

FRENCHY: This better be worth it, dumbo. Now tell me. Come on, I ain't got all day. Gonna take you long enough to say it. What's the secret?

YELLOW: C-cr-crackers.

FRENCHY: Crackers?

YELLOW: Crackers... w-white people.

FRENCHY: What about them?

YELLOW: They coming.

SCENE FOUR

OBADIAH: In the hood when you got something everybody wants a piece. "Just lemme touch, man. Just lemme hold it for a while, man. I just wanna feel it, smell
it, taste it, own it. Come on, man! Lemme borrow it fo'
a second! I'll bring it right back!" Gimme, gimme,
gimme is the ghetto anthem. My family was the first in
our neighborhood. The first to have central air-
conditioning. The first to have lawn sprinklers. The
first to have an encyclopedia set. Oh yeah. Ghetto fabu-
lous, that's us. We were nigger rich and cracker poor as
my cousins would say. So when we were the first to get
a VCR, people lined up. And when we learned how to
record something on it, the time had arrived. Because
this is 1984, and the kids on my block only cared about
one man.

*(LIGHTS SHIFT. OBADIAH's neck starts twitching like a
zombie and he's joined by FRENCHY and RED. They all
do a quick series of dance steps like monsters. Frenchy
and Red exit. OBADIAH continues to bob, grabs his
crotch and unleashes a MJ-esque…)*

OBADIAH: HOOOOO!!! *(LIGHT SHIFT BACK)* But
I'm getting ahead of myself. All the kids would come
to see, "Thriller." That was the neighborhood activity,
the daily event for us. Thriller at Obie's home. We never got tired of it. The tape played again and again. Re-
winding to the beginning…

FRENCHY (O/S): Obie-

OBADIAH: -fast forwarding to a part we liked-

FRENCHY: *(entering)* -OBIE!

OBADIAH: Quiet, Frenchy. I'm reminiscing.

FRENCHY: But we got a problem.

OBADIAH: What?

FRENCHY: White people.

OBADIAH: Excuse me?

FRENCHY: They're coming for us. Moving in and taking over. I'm scared. Hold me! *(she clutches him)* That's better.

OBADIAH: Ahhh…Frenchy.

FRENCHY: Yes, Obie.

OBADIAH: Who told you that white people were moving in?

FRENCHY: Yellow did.

OBADIAH: But Yellow is, like… retarded. Brother is so stupid I told him we got a new color TV and he asked 'what color?' You can't believe what he tells you.

FRENCHY: He's never wrong. Kiss me.

OBADIAH: What?!? *(removes her)* Wait a minute. Where are these alleged White people?

FRENCHY: Down the street, near the canal. Where is you going?

OBADIAH: I'm going to go see for myself.

FRENCHY: But you might get hurt! Aren't you scared?

OBADIAH: Why would I be scared? I see White people all the time on TV.

SCENE FIVE

(Stakeout. OBADIAH and Yellow lay on the ground. OBA-DIAH cups his hands into a pair of binoculars and scans the horizon back and forth. Yellow steals one of Obadiah's hands and looks through it, and they scan the horizon as Obadiah talks.)

OBADIAH: We're scared of what we don't know, right? Space aliens, Big Foot, Hamburger Helper and white people. I mean this is Opa-Locka. A city of blacks built in the swamps of Seminole country. A community dreamed up by a demented real estate developer who had an obsession with "One Thousand and One Nights" and an Arab fetish. Opa Locka has the largest collection of Moorish architecture in the western hemisphere. Blacks, Seminoles, Arabs, Moors. We are a tattered village of outcast people, ideas and history. We relate to Michael Jackson. A poor boy from Gary, Indiana with a fat nose, goofy grin and high voice. We live his life and see this outsider become the ultimate insider. You live as an outcasts, a minority and then one day...

(JACK enters.)

OBADIAH: ...the majority arrives at your door. They have everything and you have nothing, so what do they want with your small little community? But you shouldn't be rude or make them feel uncomfortable.

(LIGHTS SHIFT.)

OBADIAH: What are you doing here?

JACK: Hi, I'm new in the neighborhood.

OBADIAH: Why?

JACK: Why?

OBADIAH: Yes, why?

JACK: Because my parents moved here. Hi, I'm Wes.

OBADIAH: No, you're not.

JACK: I'm not?

OBADIAH: No, that's not your name.

JACK: Yes it is.

OBADIAH: The neighborhood's been talking and we've decided that your name is Jack. That's your new name, Jack.

JACK: But everyone calls me Wes.

OBADIAH: No, they don't. Everyone calls you Jack, Jack.

JACK: Why?

OBADIAH: No one told us your name, so someone just started calling you Jack and it stuck. *(to audience)* They actually called him Cracker Jack…don't look at me. I didn't come up with it. *(to JACK)* So now everyone calls you Jack, and it's going to be a pretty hard name to shake.

JACK: But I just got here.

OBADIAH: Your name arrived ahead of you. I'm Obie. This is Yellow.

JACK: Is that his real name?

OBADIAH: I don't know. Is that your real name? *(Yellow shrugs)* Well that's what we call him.

YELLOW: M-m-my b-brother is Red.

OBADIAH: Red and Yellow are twins.

JACK: *(to OBADIAH)* Oh... he's a little... slow.

OBADIAH: Slow? No, he's very fast. He's just retarded. Him and his brother. Only difference is Yellow stutters.

JACK: That's so sad.

OBADIAH: Sad my ass. They're both thieves.

YELLOW: Nu-no, w-we ain't.

OBADIAH: Oh yeah, then where's my BMX?

YELLOW: Red's got it.

OBADIAH: And then I got to Red and he says Yellow's got it. This is what they do.

JACK: Then you should call the police.

OBADIAH: The police? Jack, what the hell is wrong with you? I said I wanted my bike back. I didn't say I wanted him killed.

JACK: No, the police don't kill people. My dad said they help people fix their problems.

(YELLOW and OBADIAH look at each other and then to the audience.)

OBADIAH: You see how strange Jack is? But I'll be nice. *(to JACK)* Jack, your dad is a liar.

JACK: So now you're calling my Dad a liar?

OBADIAH: Well yeah.

(YELLOW and OBADIAH laugh at him. Jack looks at them.)

JACK: I guess I'm outnumbered.

OBADIAH: Get used to it.

JACK: *(humming)* ...'helpless like a baby.'

OBADIAH: What?

JACK: You know, the song...'looking in the mirror... helpless like a baby. I can't help it.'

OBADIAH: Michael Jackson.

JACK: Yeah. I love Michael Jackson.

OBADIAH: Are you serious?

JACK: I would give my pinkie finger for a signed album.

OBADIAH: No, you wouldn't. I'd give both my thumbs for all his signed albums.

JACK: Your thumbs? That's it?

OBADIAH: I would cut off my arm for a jacket.

JACK: I would cut off both arms for his jacket.

OBADIAH: Then how would you wear it?

JACK: I'd have the jacket stitched to my back.

OBADIAH: Wow... you've thought about this.

JACK: Michael Jackson is amazing. I'm, like, his biggest fan.

FRENCHY: *(entering quickly)* Waitwaitwaitwaitwaitwaitwaitwaitwait... Okay... um Jack, sweetie. You are not Michael Jackson's biggest fan. I am Michael Jackson's biggest fan. I am president of THE Michael Jackson fan club...I have all the albums. I write letters, I cut out all his pictures from Ebony and Jet and hang them on my wall.

JACK: Who are you?

OBADIAH: This is Frenchy.

JACK: Are all you all related?

OBADIAH: Ewwww. No, we're just all united by our devotion to Michael Jackson. It's kind of scary.

FRENCHY: Yeah, I am MJ's biggest fan. And Obie is second because he is co-founder and treasurer of the club.

JACK: Okay, well I just really like Michael Jackson. As much as you guys.

FRENCHY: You can't like him as much as us.

JACK: Why not?

OBADIAH: Frenchy, let's not get into this. Jack-

FRENCHY: Because he is our's.

JACK: ...wait... are you guys... related to Michael Jackson?!? Oh my God!! Oh my God, you do kind of look like him a little. I mean the hair, the skin-

FRENCHY: -he's ours because he's black.

JACK: So?

FRENCHY: So there is a difference. I can love... Obie, name something white...

OBADIAH: Hockey!

FRENCHY: Name something else.

OBADIAH: Ummm... serial killers! Sally Fields? Larry Bird.

FRENCHY: Perfect! So I can love Larry Bird. But I can't love him more than tall white dudes. It's different.

JACK: But when the Celtics beat the Lakers this year everyone on TV was celebrating.

FRENCHY: Nah, people were happy. But it was different. Blacks were like 'yah. Good game.' and white people were like 'FUCKING AMAZING, DUDE! Radical!' And Mexican didn't know what to do. They just looked confused. It was different. Bird was doing it for all them tall white dudes who can't dunk and wear ties to work.

JACK: Well I was rooting for the Lakers. I like Magic Johnson better any way. He's way cooler.

OBADIAH: See Frenchy! He likes Magic better than Bird.

FRENCHY: Yeah he's a regular Abraham Lincoln. 'Sho glad massa is so nice to us. I'se go tell the others.'

(FRENCHY and Yellow laugh and exit.)

JACK: Why did she talk like that?

OBADIAH: It's just 'fake slave' speech. All blacks are required to learn how to do it.

JACK: Oh, do you learn it to honor your people?

OBADIAH: No, it's usually to make fun of your people.

JACK: Everyone is so mean. I thought neighbors are supposed to welcome you when you're new in town.

OBADIAH: Look... we're just messing with you. Look, you can come over to my house tomorrow... if you like...

JACK: Umm... why?

OBADIAH: My parents have a VCR and we can watch... are you ready? "Thriller!"

JACK: And then we can hang out?

OBADIAH: Yeah. We'll 'hang'

JACK: Awesome, I've made my first friend.

OBADIAH: Sure.

JACK: Maybe we'll best buddies.

OBADIAH: We'll see.

JACK: And you'll call me Wes?

OBADIAH: Not a chance, Jack.

JACK: *(exiting)* ...at least I tried.

OBADIAH: Keep trying. *(to audience)* After that first
meeting, I told Frenchy to be nicer to Jack. Now what
we did to him was unfair, manipulative and a little cru-
el. But all the black kids I knew acted this way toward
white kids. We knew it didn't matter if we made them
squirm, because this was our way –at least for a few
years- of evening the score a little. Besides, they would
have the rest of their lives to take their revenge out on
us. And they would.

(FRENCHY and RED are on the steps outside Obadiah's home.)

RED: I wonder what he got in that house. You know crackers get all the new shit when it comes out. I bet they got a lot of nice shit in that big fancy house.

FRENCHY: He ain't no motherfucking pharaoh. He's just another Howdy Doody-looking cracker. Besides, he can't be all that if he's living here.

RED: I saw the movers carrying in a black box. You know what it said? A-T-A-R-I.

FRENCHY: You lying.

RED: They got an Atari in there. Probably the 2600.

FRENCHY: Only rich folks got the 2600.

RED: He's probably playing Space Invaders in there right now.

FRENCHY: Space Invaders?

RED: Yeah, like an arcade. And he's probably got Pong and Frogger,

FRENCHY: You dreaming. You think he's got it like that?

RED: Slinks said he got a white boy moved in next door and they got Donkey Kong in there house. And dat E.T. game in the arcade.

FRENCHY: The E.T. arcade game sucked. Besides, my mom's got a Commodore at work and she said in a few years they may let us have it.

RED: You broke-ass Africans don't even have a toaster. How you gonna get a Commodore?

FRENCHY: We don't have a toaster cuz your stupid-ass brother tried to toast crayons in it.

RED: He was trying to make a rainbow.

(JACK enters. Frenchy tries to be nice but is rolling her eyes and looking at him suspiciously.)

FRENCHY: Hey, Jack.

JACK: Hi, French.

FRENCHY: It's Frenchy.

JACK: Oh, like in "Grease"?

FRENCHY: What? No, like in Paris, France.

RED: What's happening, Jackie? Ain't it funny how life is like Space Invaders?

JACK: I don't understand.

RED: You been playing video games in there, haven't you?

JACK: No.

RED: Let me see your fingers.

FRENCHY: Don't mind Red. We're trying to get him to switch to a different race. Something a little less embarrassing for our people.

RED: Frenchy, his finger tips are hard. He's playing video games!

FRENCHY: Ignore the felon. Look I'm sorry about what I said earlier. We wanted to welcome you into our club... if you were interested in joining.

JACK: Sure. I got a lot of cool Michael Jackson stuff we can do. We can have a dance party. Buy gloves and put glitter on them-

FRENCHY: -that's great, but all MJ related activities have to run through me. But first we have to ask you a few questions. An entrance exam we give it to all of the members.

JACK: Wow, an exam. It sounds so official. Is there anything I should do to prepare-

FRENCHY: -first question. Michael Jackson was born where?

JACK: That's easy. Gary, Indiana.

FRENCHY: How many Jackson kids?

JACK: 9.

FRENCHY: 10.

JACK: Shoot. But Michael was the 8th.

FRENCHY: No, he was the 7th.

OBADIAH: *(entering)* He was the 8th. Everyone getting along?

FRENCHY: Yeah. Just getting to know Jack a little better.

JACK: They're giving me the entrance exam into your club.

OBADIAH: Entrance exam? We don't have-

FRENCHY: -Next question. What was the Jackson 5's first hit?

JACK: Easy. "I Want You Back."

FRENCHY: First solo hit?

JACK: Umm...

FRENCHY: ...ah-ha! I thought so! "Don't Stop Till You Get Enough!"

JACK: ...no it wasn't.

FRENCHY: Yeah it was Jack. I told you, you don't love him like I do.

JACK: It was "You Can't Win." From "The Wiz."

FRENCHY: What?

OBADIAH: He's right. "The Wiz" did come out before that.

FRENCHY: Wait... okay... movie soundtracks don't count.

JACK: You didn't say that.

FRENCHY: Well I'm saying it now.

OBADIAH: All right. Enough. We're here today for "Thriller." Who wants to see it?

(Everyone scream. Jack stands up and starts dancing excitedly.)

FRENCHY: Sit your cracker ass down!

(Jack stops dancing.)

OBADIAH: Frenchy, remember: nice.

FRENCHY: I'm sorry. Jack, please sit your cracker ass down.

(Jack sits down.)

OBADIAH: Thank you. Now before we get to "Thriller" I have an even bigger surprise: a meeting.

(Frenchy and Red boo.)

OBADIAH: As your treasurer I went down and asked about the mural costs and they said someone has agreed to donate the entire amount. We don't have to ask for any money or dig into our savings, which is good because we only have about 37 cents left out of the founder's initial dollar.

FRENCHY: Obie that's great! You are so brilliant, I knew you would be perfect as treasurer of my fan club. How did you get-

OBADIAH: -We got an angel donor.

FRENCHY: From who?

OBADIAH: Jack.

FRENCHY: What?

JACK: My Dad said he could get his company to put up the difference.

OBADIAH: There's just one thing though…

FRENCHY: Thank you, Jack. I was wrong about you. You're in the club for sure. I'll even make you an honorary board member. This is great!!

OBADIAH: Frenchy, there's a catch though-

FRENCHY: Oh, who cares?!? As long as it gets done!

OBADIAH: I'm glad you feel that way. Cause Jack gets to organize the project.

FRENCHY: What?

OBADIAH: He thought it was only fair that since he was helping to pay for it, his son -Wesley- should be entitled to help put it together.

FRENCHY: But... that was my job.

RED: Who cares! As long as it gets done. That's what you said French.

OBADIAH: Frenchy it's gonna be a great mural. And Jack is a nice guy. He likes Michael Jackson. He knows all the trivia.

JACK: "I Got You/I Feel Good." That was the song the Jacksons performed that won them their first talent show competition. It's by James Brown, who is also very cool.

FRENCHY: But new guys can't just come in and takeover stuff. We got rules here about board members.

OBADIAH: Frenchy, you ever heard of the Golden Rule?

FRENCHY: No.

OBADIAH: He who has the gold, makes the rules.

FRENCHY: Well the board still has to vote on it.

OBADIAH: Okay. All those against this? *(Frenchy raises her hand)* All those for it *(Red and Jack raise hand).* And all those staying the hell out of it *(Obadiah raises his hand).* It passes. Congratulations Jack. Now for Thriller.

JACK: I can't wait to get started on this.

(Jack and Obadiah exit. Frenchy sits outside stewing while Red teases her.)

RED: What's the matter Frenchy? You sweating like a Haitian now. And if you keep it up, your hair gonna nap up like an African. You don't have to worry. In the movie, the White zombies eat your brains first. And since you ain't got no brains, you should be cool for a while. Hehehe. BAM!

SCENE SEVEN

(FRENCHY talks to friends in the fan club.)

FRENCHY: So this White boy comes in and starts messing things up. First day he takes my seat in Obie's living room for "Thriller." I mean, this is Frenchy Clark's seat. Ain't nooo-body supposed to sit in that seat. He just comes in like he's God/king all-mighty. And nobody stops him. Not even Obie. See, folks, this is how it starts. This is how white people take over. My momma told me all about it. First it's your seat, then it's the whole neighborhood. They're all sitting in there, laughing and jumping like it's the first time they've seen it. Trying to impress Cracker Jack. Like he's special. But what about Frenchy Carter? I'm the special one. Shoo, they make me sick.

(Frenchy continues miming her diatribe as the LIGHTS SHIFT and RED enters. He stands next to Frenchy. Spotlight on him. NOTE: in this exchange Yellow and Red are on opposite shoulders of Frenchy. They can be differentiated by different color shirts or baseball caps.)

RED: *(thinking)* I wonder what dem titties feel like? I heard a black woman titties are as warm as chocolate chip cookies. One big chocolate chip right in the middle of each titty. Maybe Frenchy would let me eat her chocolate chips. They in the oven, growing bigger and softer every day.

(LIGHTS SHIFT to YELLOW.)

YELLOW: *(thinking)* R-red... wa-why staring at F-Frenchy's chest? (He looks down) Dayum! S-sweet gravy. Red? R-red, I know you hear wh-what Imma thinkin'...

(LIGHTS SHIFT BACK TO RED.)

RED: Hell yeah, twin ESP. I know your thoughts. And I ain't sharing my chocolate chip cookies. Damn, this girl still talking.

FRENCHY: I can't wait till I marry Michael Jackson and move into his mansion. We'll buy this block and all of Opa Locka. What kind of a stupid name is that for a city. I'll pour gasoline on all the roofs and burn down this whole city and rename it "French Toast," which will be the name of our first kid.

RED: That's cool, Frenchy.

FRENCHY: Ahh, Red? What are you 2 felons looking at?

YELLOW: Hu-hu-he just like your shirt.

FRENCHY: Why are you two acting so weird?

YELLOW: C-cuz, w-we-we-we l-looking at-

FRENCHY: -looking at what?

RED: Nevermind! What were you saying about Michael?

FRENCHY: Oh, and we'll have ten kids and move to Africa and buy some islands. And each island will be named after our kids.

RED: Booty thicker than a bag of Snickers.

FRENCHY: And Michael will dedicate his next album to me and I'll become famous, and everyone will know me, but I won't know anyone, like all stars.

YELLOW: Thighs s-swole like Bu-bublicious.

FRENCHY: We'll be on the cover of *Ebony* and I'll be *Jet's* swimsuit model of the week, and I'll start my own hair products line called "Kool n' Kinky" which will blowout people's hair into an afro. And I'll become president and then queen and then an astronaut, in that order.

RED: Damn those chocolate chip cookies.

FRENCHY: I'll be so famous I might have to marry another husband, Tito Jackson... maybe Jermaine. If Obie acts right, I might even let him marry me. But first Michael, I promise. And, and, and... that's what is going to happen. Yeah. Just like that.

SCENE EIGHT

(Jack watches TV and Obadiah comes into his living room.)

OBADIAH: Jack, you ready to go to Nasty Man?

JACK: What's that?

OBADIAH: The store.

JACK: You got a store called Nasty Man?

OBADIAH: Yeah. It's the one on the corner. They couldn't afford a sign when it opened so there was no name for a while. So people-

JACK: -came up with one for it. Why do you call it that?

OBADIAH: Cause it's nasty, man! Windows got dead flies stuck to the glass, toilet is always backed up. But the boiled peanuts are amazing, the grape drink is cold, and they got a Jamaican patty that'll make you cry. You should show your face there. Nasty will probably give you a free bag of peanuts.

JACK: Really? All of sudden everyone is so nice to me.

OBADIAH: That's the Golden Rule.

JACK: I don't know who to pick for the mural.

OBADIAH: Pick whoever gives you the most.

JACK: That doesn't seem fair. Maybe you can help me?

OBADIAH: Help you how?

JACK: You can tell me who to pick for the different parts.

OBADIAH: Why me?

JACK: You were the first one who wanted to hang out with me. Even my Dad likes you. He says you're not like the others and you can come over. He even said you could even sleep over and he wouldn't even be scared.

OBADIAH: Gee, thanks.

JACK: We should have a sleepover. And then you can help me pick.

OBADIAH: Why can't you just do it?

JACK: Cause everyone is so nice to me. But not in a good way. You guys are always together, laughing and having a good time.

OBADIAH: Well you got in the club so you can always join us.

JACK: It's not the same. I'm just in the club because my Dad paid me in. But I want to be like you guys. Like a family.

OBADIAH: You're too plain to be…in, Jack.

JACK: Why?

OBADIAH: Cause all of us are messed up. That's why we came together. Frenchy's dad left and her mom drinks, Red and Yellow's dad beats the hell out of them.

JACK: Well what's wrong with you?

OBADIAH: I don't know. My parents are never around. So these guys became my family.

JACK: I can be family too.

OBADIAH: Jack, you're just too normal.

JACK: No, I have messed up stuff about me.

OBADIAH: Like what?

JACK: My Dad does things and that's why we had to leave the last place we lived at. Cause of what he did.

OBADIAH: What did he do?

JACK: I don't want to talk about it. If I tell you, you'll hate me and tell other people. And then we'll have to move again. But I just was just proving that I have messed up stuff about me too.

OBADIAH: But that isn't you. That's your Dad.

JACK: ...right. You're so smart Obie. I just want every-one here to be my friend like they are with you.

OBADIAH: Why do you think most people are friends with me?

JACK: Cause you're smart and funny?

OBADIAH: It's because I have a VCR.

JACK: That's not the only reason.

OBADIAH: Sure and we got stuff that people take. Got a mango tree in the backyard and I haven't tasted one mango from it. Why? Cause before the mangos get ripe, people peel back our fence at night and pluck the tree bald.

JACK: Frenchy likes you. A lot of the girls like you.

OBADIAH: Cause I'm high yellow.

JACK: Cause you're what?

OBADIAH: Nevermind. Look, why don't we go to Nasty Man. Get some free boiled peanuts, grape drink and go over to my place and watch "Thriller"

JACK: But no one else is over there.

OBADIAH: I'll show it just for you. Payback for the glove. A private viewing of "Thriller."

JACK: Oh... sure, okay.

OBADIAH: What's wrong?

JACK: I've seen "Thriller." Many, many times.

OBADIAH: How?

JACK: I have the tape.

OBADIAH: What?!?

JACK: I'm sorry, I was going to tell you, but my parents have a VCR. BETA. You should switch. My dad says it's the future.

OBADIAH: You had a VCR this whole time?

JACK: Yeah, my Dad keeps it hidden because he's afraid... well he just likes to keep stuff hidden. And I didn't want to say anything.

OBADIAH: Great.

JACK: I just wanted to fit in.

OBADIAH: With us poor kids, right?

JACK: No! With you. I thought you wouldn't talk to me, or... or...

OBADIAH: Or what?

JACK: Be my pal. You know, a special friend.

OBADIAH: *(to audience)* At this moment, a strange feeling is bubbling up. A chemical reaction like... something coming loose and breaking a part. My mom makes a special stew out of chopped carrots, sliced onions, diced celery, and beef chuck. Hours of stirring the pot and the meat would break apart into thin, stringy fibers of flesh until it was unrecognizable. And things inside me keep bubbling up, breaking apart, disintegrating, and falling down. This hot gray stew is in my gut. Rising up my chest and neck, up through my head. Bubbling and foaming over the brim and sliding down the sides of me.

(JACK pumps his fists and OBADIAH jerks away.)

JACK: Ah. You flinched!

(Jack punches him three times on the arm and then rubs it.)

JACK: Your turn.

(OBADIAH looks at the floor. He raises his fists slowly and suddenly jerks forward. JACK flinches.)

JACK: I flinched. Now you hit me.

(OBADIAH raises his arm but can't bring it down. There's a strange moment: intimate and tender. Obadiah breaks the moment by jokingly punching Jack and laughing.)

OBADIAH: You're funny.

JACK: *(runs off)* Hey, you wanna see something?

OBADIAH: What? You got an Atari back there, don't you? Everyone's said they've seen the box.

JACK: *(O/S)* That's all I have left. My Dad traded it in.

OBADIAH: Jack, your father should be arrested! How do you trade in an Atari? It's got Frogger!

JACK: *(re-enters with VCR tape)* I know but the salesman convinced him to buy something else. It's this weird Japanese thing. You gotta keep this a secret, ok?

OBADIAH: I better cause if I tell kids you gave away Atari, you'd lose all your cool points.

JACK: No, that's not the big secret. This is. *(shows tape)*

OBADIAH: Is that your copy of *Thriller*?

JACK: No. Look, my dad would kill me if he found this outside his stash. You can't tell anyone.

OBADIAH: All right, Jeez! Just put it in.

JACK: I don't want to show it to you now. You should come back. Let's have a sleepover.

OBADIAH: To watch a video?

JACK: Yeah, try something new, right? We can talk, hang out, and watch this. It should be watched at night.

SCENE NINE

(Pieced-together mural of Michael Jackson's face.)

OBADIAH: We were going to use a picture of Michael Jackson from "Off the Wall" and let people in the neighborhood just decorate it. The designer Jack's Dad hired said we could make a mosaic. Little pieces of Michael that each person could take away and add something to and bring back. That way everyone gets to do something. But then people started to fight over who got what, so Jack had to take over. He handed them out to people.

(Pieces of the mural disappear.)

OBADIAH: The ears were the first to go. Then the neck, hair, chin. Jack said he wanted to save the bigger parts for the bigger friends. Nasty Man gave him free boiled peanuts for a week. He puts them in this wet paper bag and Jack said it looked disgusting. The peanuts were all slimy and wet. Nasty Man had these red eyes, and his breath smelled. He had sores on his arms and he told Jack that he works on the weekend as a lawn man and that he does the lawns in half the neighborhood. The peanuts were good so Jack gave Nasty's son the nose. Frenchy got an eyebrow. I know she's the president of the fan club and all, but until she learns to be nicer to Jack that's all he's giving her.

SCENE TEN

(Frenchy talks with Yellow about how everything has gone wrong. Yellow tries to seduce her.)

FRENCHY: I call this emergency meeting of "The Opa Locka, Florida and Miami-Dade County Michael Jackson Fan Club" to order. I just want to say that we have a serious issue and that issue is Cracker Jack and how he's taken over this club.

YELLOW: W-whut you talkin' 'bout?

FRENCHY: Yellow we can't let these white folks take over. They're like aliens. But not the cool E.T kind. Now Cracker Jack-er has taken over. And that was my project! It ain't fair.

YELLOW: T-t-t-t-tough.

FRENCHY: Tough?

YELLOW: T-t-tough. Dat's what they do.

FRENCHY: And are you gonna just sit there and stand for it? We need to strike back.

YELLOW: *(singing softly to her)* You can't win. You can't break even. And you can't get out of the game.

(Yellow tries to kiss her. Frenchy ignores him and blocks his kiss with a sudden epiphany.)

FRENCHY: Let's vote him outta the club! Then we go down and talk to Opa Locka city manager and tell him Cracker Jack ain't a part of the club no more so he can't be in charge. I'll start up a petition to get him off the board. Just gotta come up with a catchy title, sign it, then get your brother to sign it, then some of my friends...

YELLOW: Wh-hut about Obie?

FRENCHY: He'll come around. And you'll use them claws of yours and scribble your name.

(BEAT)

FRENCHY: What's the matter?

YELLOW: J-jack has Atari. Obie t-told m-me he played it.

FRENCHY: So? Yellow, you gonna let Atari get in the way of our friendship?

YELLOW: Yup.

FRENCHY: Fine! Go on with ya' retarded ass. Probably can't even play the game. Sell your own sister down the river for a game. You see, dat's what dem white folks want you to do, Yellow. My mom used to be in wit' dem Black Panthers and she told me all about how dem white folks trick no-education-having niggers with penny candy and a smile. My momma knows all about dat.

YELLOW: J-just cuz y-yo momma so B-Black she pur-ple d-don't make her a Black Panther.

FRENCHY: You just another house nigger.

YELLOW: W-what?

FRENCHY: A house nigger. You selling me out for Atari so you can sit up in Jack's house smiling crooked as the devil while he lets you play his games for a few minutes. I don't need you cause Obie's gonna back me up with this. And so are a lot of other kids. So go on with your stupid games.

YELLOW: *(exiting)* M-maybe retarded, b-but I ain't stupid, Frenchy.

FRENCHY: You can't let White people just take over stuff without a fight. They coming for me and all of you. They coming for the aliens, for Michael Jackson, for all of it. But I'm not gonna let them. Look at what happened to Lionel Richie! And Debarge! They get in the mix and get ya to switch.

SCENE ELEVEN

(Jack and Obie play Nintendo.)

OBADIAH: Jack, I was thinking about the painting?

JACK: Yeah?

OBADIAH: How about we do something nice for Frenchy?

JACK: What do you mean?

OBADIAH: I noticed you haven't given away a few pieces. You still got the eyes.

JACK: I'm saving the eyes. They're special.

OBADIAH: What's so special about them?

JACK: The eyes are the center. Everybody wants them.

OBADIAH: I just feel bad since the whole thing was sort of Frenchy's idea.

JACK: Why do you care about her?

OBADIAH: Cause she's my friend. And she's cool. You guys should be friends.

JACK: Every time I see her I try to say hi but she just turns her nose up and walks off. That's not a friend. You're my friend.

OBADIAH: Well… thanks.

JACK: You wanna see something?

OBADIAH: What?

JACK: The video. But remember….

45

OBADIAH: …yeah, secret. Sure. Fine.

JACK: Cool.

(Jack stops playing Nintendo and exits. Obadiah pauses the game.)

OBADIAH: Jack rummaged under his bed and then came out with this black BETA tape and a quilt. He looked like he was carrying a grenade and put them down gently. I started to shiver.

JACK: Are you cold?

OBADIAH: A little.

JACK: *(handing him quilt)* Here.

OBADIAH: *(wrapping self in quilt)* Thanks. Then Jack put in the tape.

JACK: *(getting under quilt)* It's kind of fuzzy at first. I don't know if you can see it.

OBADIAH: Kind of… what is that? An elbow? A chin?

JACK: It takes a minute to come into focus.

OBADIAH: Okay, I see a man and a woman and…

JACK: Yeah.

OBADIAH: That's their skin. All of it.

JACK: Yeah.

OBADIAH: And they look very… very… angry. No. No, I take that back. They look… I don't know what they look like.

JACK: Isn't it cool?

OBADIAH: It feels like the room got 30 degrees colder.

JACK: My Dad said it's the real reason people started buying VCRs. So they could watch… 'this.'

OBADIAH: How did you get 'this?'

JACK: He ordered it from a catalog. It came in this package in the mail wrapped in brown paper like my school lunch. And he told me he had to hide it from my mom because she would get pissed if she saw it. So I hid it under my bed and then… when she was gone to the store a few days ago, we watched it.

OBADIAH: With your Dad?

JACK: Yeah, it's cool right? Everyone does this when they grow up. Makes you wanna grow up faster. Hey, are you all right?

OBADIAH: Huh?

JACK: You're not freaking out, are you? Cause we said we'd keep this a secret. My Dad can't find out I showed this to you.

OBADIAH: I won't tell.

JACK: Do you want me to turn it off?

OBADIAH: …no.

(Obadiah is transfixed at the screen. Jack inches closer.)

JACK: Hey Obie? Can I feel your hair?

OBADIAH: My hair?

JACK: Yeah, it looks different.

OBADIAH: Little did I know that for decades this would be a constant question every time I ran into whites. I know they're curious but it makes me feel like I'm in a zoo. They ask and then they put their fingers on it. Some squeal with delight at the experience, others are fascinated and begin running their fingers over my scalp. And you kind of just stand or sit there as someone is touching you. But not like a person. It never feels like they're touching me. It's like they're pressing their fingers in me and I leave. My hair, my skin, my whole body. And I feel like I'm standing somewhere else watching them say...

JACK: Wow, it feels like a brillo pad. I wonder what Michael Jackson's hair feels like?

OBADIAH: Probably wet. He's got a jheri curl. A lot of activator juice.

JACK: You're funny. I feel like when you're talking to kids, you're talking over them, sort of making fun of them. My mom says that means you're probably real smart. Are you black?

OBADIAH: Yeah.

JACK: But all of you? It's just that my parents were wondering if your family was half of something. Like a Cuban or Seminole.

OBADIAH: Nope. Just black.

JACK: Really? Like forever?

OBADIAH: Okay, I think my Mom said we're part Irish.

JACK: Like Larry Bird.

OBADIAH: No, like a leprechaun. But that's a zillion years ago.

JACK: That's so cool. So you're like me.

OBADIAH: No. I'm black.

JACK: I wish I was part black. But not too black. Not like Nasty Man or Frenchy. Just enough so I could… I wish I was Black like you. Or Michael Jackson.

OBADIAH: Well I wish you were too, Jack.

JACK: Obie, I like you. Do you like me?

OBADIAH: You're… sure, Jack. I like you.

JACK: I wanna show you something my Dad showed me. Can I?

OBADIAH: Sure. Fine.

(Sound of static rising as Jack and Obadiah go under the covers. The world goes into darkness except for the eyes on the mural.)

END OF ACT ONE

ACT TWO

SCENE ONE

RED: RIOT!!!!

(Police sirens and helicopters buzz as a riot unfolds. Red and Frenchy talk to the audience. Their words overlap.)

RED: Every two years it's like clockwork. Christmas in the summer. Time to go shopping!

FRENCHY: In 1980 it was Arthur McDuffie. A Black man was beaten to death by 12 white police officers at a traffic stop. In 1982 it was a black kid shot and killed at a video arcade by a white cop. The pig said he thought the black kid was trying to reach for a gun. Come on, man! Has you never been in a video arcade before?

RED: Riots are like Christmas. Except you your own Santa Claus.

FRENCHY: It's disgusting how these idiots cut up. In the summer, after hurricanes. And especially around Halloween.

RED: Get whatcha want! Get whatcha need!

FRENCHY: See, this is why we can't have nothing. This is why we can't move forward.

RED: I'm moving this toaster forward, bitch! Brother Red is getting fed. Ahahaha!

FRENCHY: You guys are a disgrace! Stop it! You're only hurting yourself. What about the Black community?

RED: Fuck them! What they do for me, huh? Call me and my brother retarded, stick us in the back of the class. Call us stupid and make us ride the little bus. Kids laughing at us, teachers beating our asses. But we gotta go so my dad can collect his check. Getting our asses beat for 10 years so I can go work at the post office. Fuck that shit. Me and my brother not big enough to get the real prizes during a riot. Mostly when you're a kid you gotta crawl around. Wait for the gangs and the ex-cons to get their share. Then it's the pissed-off Dads and Moms who got bats and guns they wanna use. Then we crawl in. Snatch the small stuff, some food, maybe a can opener, some batteries, toaster. Yellow found me a tape deck. Guess what it's got in it? "Off the Wall." The classic.

FRENCHY: What would Jesse Jackson say? Or Malcolm X?

RED: *(listening to tape)* Who? Well I ain't never met them niggas but I'm pretty sure they'd say 'get your's cause Imma get mine.'

FRENCHY: What would Michael Jackson say?

RED: He'd say "Don't Stop 'Till You Get Enough."

FRENCHY: What would the Jackson 5 say?

RED: I think I saw Tito and Jermaine around the corner carrying a dish washer.

FRENCHY: Michael would tell us to love each other. He'd say we gotta stop the violence-

RED: -"Burn This Disco Out…"

FRENCHY: If we don't stop you know what's gonna happen next?

RED: "I wanna rock wit' you. SLAP. All night! Feel you in the-

FRENCHY: -guns. They're gonna start firing in the air!

(GUNFIRE erupts in the air.)

RED: Ghetto fireworks!

(They scramble and run into each other.)

FRENCHY: Red! They're lighting up the sky again.

RED: I know. It's kind of cool. "I can't help it... if I wanted to. I can't help it... if I tried..."

FRENCHY: Red, what is wrong with you?

RED: *(flirting)* Hey, you wanna go up on the roof and try to see the tracers?

FRENCHY: What?!? No, Red! The bullets come down, jackass!

RED: Frenchy, how come you always so mean to me? My brother, I understand, but me?

FRENCHY: Red, you acting strange.

RED: *(taking out marijuana blunt and smoking)* One of the bums gave me something to celebrate.

FRENCHY: Red, you in the 6th grade. Twice. You're not allowed to get high.

RED: Not allowed to do a lot of things.

FRENCHY: Oooooh, Imma tell yo daddy.

RED: Frenchy, my whole head feels like it's floating. I gotta get some more of this.

FRENCHY: You're going to feel like shit tomorrow.

RED: It's beautiful. Why can't you be happy for me?

FRENCHY: My momma says every time you get high you lose a couple of brain cells. What are you gonna do, boy? You're already slow. Now you gonna add slow and high?

RED: Frenchy, why are you like that? You should be nice to me, girl. You should start being nice to me.

FRENCHY: *(backing up)*: Okay, Red. I'll try.

RED: How about you start trying now…

(Red kisses and gropes Frenchy. She punches him in the face.)

FRENCHY: Muthafucka what's wrong with you?

RED: That's all right. *(standing up)* You ugly any way.

FRENCHY: Just go home Red.

RED: Dark, midnight-looking-gorilla black bitch-

FRENCHY: GO HOME!!

RED: You stupid, Frenchy. What you saving them good-ies for? Ain't nobody gonna love you. What, you waiting on MJ to marry you?

FRENCHY: You don't know anything.

RED: Or maybe you waiting for that red-boned faggot to kiss you.

FRENCHY: What?

RED: "What?!?" Ahaha, you think Obie's ever gonna touch you? You been holding out for a faggot all this time. Now who's retarded?!?

FRENCHY: You're lying, Red. You're a liar.

(Frenchy hits Red, who laughs. He stands with his arm wide open, daring her.)

RED: What you got, huh? Come on, bitch. What you gonna do?

(Frenchy unloads on him with punches and slaps. Red stands there like a rock.)

RED: *(as he's getting hit)* That it? That all you got for me, Frenchy? Huh, come on. When you're done it's my turn. When you're done it's my turn, bitch. You better knock me out, Frenchy. Imma beat that face and that pussy when you're done so you better knock me out. Imma tax that gorilla pussy. Come on with it!

(Frenchy stops hitting him. Red moves toward her. He fakes like he's going to punch her and she flinches. He laughs.)

FRENCHY: Red-

RED: Shhhhh... one of these days Frenchy... *(looks her up and down)* It'll be real quiet. You won't even see it coming and then... snatch! Hell, you might even like it. Beg for it. You know why? Cause.

(BEAT)

RED: Nobody's gonna ever love you, girl.

(Red wanders off. More gunfire and Frenchy screams. She runs over to Obadiah's place.)

SCENE TWO

(Frenchy knocks. Obadiah answers the door.)

OBADIAH: Frenchy what's wrong?

FRENCHY: My mom's not home and I got locked out. Can I...

OBADIAH: Yeah sure. You ok?

(They walk into the house.)

FRENCHY: Nah... nope, I'm cool. I just want some place to hang out for a bit...

OBADIAH: In the middle of a riot?

FRENCHY: Yeah.

OBADIAH: It's all right to be scared. It's pretty scary-

FRENCHY: -I ain't scar'red. Okay? Are you scared?

OBADIAH: Yeah.

FRENCHY: You're not supposed to say that, Obie. You're supposed to be a strong black man and say you ain't scared of anything. That everything'll be okay.

OBADIAH: Who told you that mess?

FRENCHY: My mom.

OBADIAH: Not your Dad?

FRENCHY: Obie, you know my dad left when I was 5.

OBADIAH: He was probably scared.

FRENCHY: He needed to be a man and take care of his business. That's what he needed to do. What is wrong with black folk?

OBADIAH: I think we're all scared.

FRENCHY: Stop saying that shit, Obie!

(BEAT)

FRENCHY: Scared of what, white people?

OBADIAH: Remember when I was going to that fancy private school with all them white kids?

FRENCHY: Ugh. Yes. Your sister went there too long and became uppity and all *(imitating stuck-up rich woman)* 'oh, how are YOU doing today, mother?' Stuck-up, siddity little-

OBADIAH: -Okay, okay, I get it. No one would want to be my study partner, or work on projects together. But I was the first to be picked on all the teams.

FRENCHY: So what?

OBADIAH: Before anyone knew me. And they never got to know me. It was like 'here's the prize. Talented pet.' Who's going to get to take him out? And I would just say 'Sure. Fine.' Kids, thought I was tough because I was Black and didn't say many words. But I didn't say anything at that school because I was scared that if they got to know me...if they really knew what was inside...

FRENCHY: And what is inside, Obie?

OBADIAH: ...I don't know. That became my nickname: SureFine. Cause I said it so much. I didn't even have my own name any more. Like those kids the cops shoot down in the street every summer. It's like they don't even have names any more.

56

FRENCHY: Well when you get married –to a Black woman- and raise your kids, they'll been seen and have beautiful names like Africa and Kenyatta.

OBADIAH: We'll see.

FRENCHY: Obie, you are getting married to a Black woman!

OBADIAH: Sure… fine.

FRENCHY: And not everyone is scared. You know who isn't scared?

OBADIAH: *(sighing)* Michael Jackson.

FRENCHY: Exactly! Hanging around Cracker Jack is making you soft.

OBADIAH: He says 'hi' by the way.

FRENCHY: Yeah right.

(Yellow walks in eating from a bag of food. Obadiah is startled.)

OBADIAH: Yellow! Stop walking in my house unannounced. You scared the shit outta me.

YELLOW: Sorry.

OBADIAH: Well, I see you've been having a good time.

YELLOW: Yeah, w-went shopping. You w-want some?

FRENCHY: We don't eat stolen food around here, Yellow! And when is this shooting gonna stop?!? Sometimes I hate black people.

OBADIAH: How can you hate your own family?

FRENCHY: When your family betrays you it's easy. By the way... how's the Atari?

OBADIAH: How would we know?

FRENCHY: I thought Jack and you all be playing Atari all the time. That's what Red be saying.

OBADIAH: Jack doesn't have an Atari. He has an NES.

FRENCHY: What?

YELLOW: Nin-ni-ni-

OBADIAH: It's coming soon...

FRENCHY: I'm gonna be dead by the time he gets this out...

YELLOW: Ni-ni... Nintendo. It's Japanese.

FRENCHY: Japanese?!? Sounds stupid. *(pause)* So Cracker Jack don't even have *Frogger* or *Pong*?

OBADIAH: Nah. But he does have *Donkey Kong*.

FRENCHY: Well lucky you.

OBADIAH: Look, Frenchy I know we don't hang out as much as we used to, but... things are changing.

FRENCHY: What's changed? I haven't changed. Yellow hasn't changed. He is still retarded. Red is still a felon and Black folks still burning down their own homes and stores. What's changed?

OBADIAH: Me.

FRENCHY: How?

YELLOW: Yeah, how?

OBADIAH: It's hard to explain.

FRENCHY: I know how you've changed. You don't got my back any more.

OBADIAH: That's cause you haven't been asking me to get your back.

YELLOW: S-sign the p-papers.

FRENCHY: Naw, forget it.

OBADIAH: What papers?

FRENCHY: I had this idea but since Red didn't back me up and nobody else did... I just gave up on it.

OBADIAH: What was the idea?

FRENCHY: I had a petition to get Jack kicked out of the club.

OBADIAH: Then everything might return to normal? Yeah, I like that.

FRENCHY/YELLOW: WHAT?!?

OBADIAH: I mean things have gotten kind of crazy, right?

FRENCHY: Yeah.

OBADIAH: And it's not Jack's fault but maybe this whole rainbow coalition, peace-and-love thing isn't gonna work.

FRENCHY: Yeah, I mean I don't have nothing against white folks.

(Obadiah and Yellow skeptically look at each and the audience.)

FRENCHY: You got, um... Abraham Lincoln, Wonder Woman, Ronald McDonald... Mrs. Buttersworth! They're cool.

OBADIAH: Sure. And maybe things would return back to the way they used to be.

YELLOW: W-what about the... Ni-ni-ni-ni...

FRENCHY: O Lawd.

OBADIAH: The Nintendo?

YELLOW: Yeah.

OBADIAH: Sorry, Yellow. But we all gotta make sacrifices.

FRENCHY: I was wrong about you. Maybe you do got a sista's back? How are we gonna kick him out?

OBADIAH: We'll just ask him.

FRENCHY: Obie, you can't just walk in white folks house and say 'hey, we'd like to take away your power.' What's wrong with you? I thought you were supposed to be the smart one.

OBADIAH: I can get Jack to do it.

FRENCHY: Well even if you could, -which I doubt- what about the Michael Jackson mural? His Dad is paying for it.

OBADIAH: Jack given away most of the pieces so it's not like his Dad can take his money back.

FRENCHY: So the fan club is back together again?

OBADIAH: Absolutely.

FRENCHY: I gotta tell my mom's. She's gonna be so happy. We are taking back Michael Jackson!

OBADIAH: I'm ready to do this.

FRENCHY: See you guys, later. And Obie, are you still scared?

OBADIAH: Girl, I ain't scared of nothing.

SCENE THREE

(A few pieces of MJ's face are brought back into the mural.)

JACK: People have already started turning in their pieces of the mural. After the riot a lot of community leaders thought this could be a fun thing to do. Unify people and bring them together. The riots were scary. And confusing. Why would people shoot and burn down their own stuff? My Dad says it's because Black people don't know any better but to act like monkeys. But I know that's not true and for the first time I stood up to him. I said 'Obie is smart. He wouldn't burn down his house.' And my Dad that's because Obie is half-white, and if he was all Black he would've been out there looting like the rest of them...' and then he said a word that I know you're not supposed to say. Even though my Mom says she likes it here, my Dad said moving here was a big mistake. And the only place to get groceries at night is Nasty Man's store and my father refuses to let her enter an establishment that has pickled pig feet floating in a jar. But if we didn't move here I would've never met Obie. He's so... my mom saw him working at the mural and said he was very articulate and very clean.

OBADIAH: *(entering)* Okay, I got us some salt n' vinegar chips, and candy apples from Nasty Man's.

JACK: Did he touch the candy apples with his hands?

OBADIAH: Afraid so.

JACK: Ew... his cooties are going to be slimed on it.

OBADIAH: It'll still taste good. Where are your parents?

JACK: My Dad is working late and my Mom had to drive across town to get milk.

OBADIAH: Why didn't she just go down a block to Nasty Man's?

JACK: I don't know. Hey Obie, I got a surprise! *(reveals tape)* Another one of my Dad's videos came in. *Behind the Green Door.* I wonder what's behind it? You wanna watch?

OBADIAH: Maybe. I think a few friends from the neighborhood wanted to stop by and talk to you Jack.

JACK: I'm tired of talking about the mural. Besides we got time. It'll be fun. You want to, right? Come on… it's just touching and I like the way you feel when I'm… when we touch.

(Jack puts in tape and grabs blanket. He drapes it over himself and Obadiah as they watch the tape. Jack and Obadiah look straight ahead as they reach for each other under the blanket.)

JACK: *(whispering)* Can I…

OBADIAH: Sure. Fine.

(Jack lifts the blanket up over their heads.)

OBADIAH: Can I…

JACK: Yes.

(The blanket shifts and squirms on the floor. YELLOW walks in eating candy. He looks at the blanket and waits. He eats and watches. Then he notices what's on the screen and becomes hypnotized.

Yellow drops some of the candy on the blanket. He picks it up, gobbles it down, and continues watching the screen.)

YELLOW: HEY! Are y-you-

(Obadiah and Jack explode from under the blanket half-clothed. They scramble around to put on clothes.)

OBADIAH: YELLOW!!!

JACK: OH SHIT! How did he get in here?

OBADIAH: He's a thief. How do you think he got in?

YELLOW: This the n-new game on Ni-ni-ni-

JACK: No, it's not Nintendo! Oh my God, if my parents find out Obie-

OBADIAH: Jack, stay cool.

JACK: He can't tell anybody.

OBADIAH: He's not. Yellow, you're not going to tell anyone right?

(Yellow shrugs his shoulders.)

JACK: What? What does that mean? Is that a 'no?' Is he saying no?

OBADIAH: He wants something.

JACK: What? You want some of my Michael Jackson tapes, Yellow? The mural! I'll give you the eyes. You can do whatever you want with it.

(Yellow shrugs his shoulder.)

JACK: Now he's got nothing to say. Do you want to wear my *Thriller* jacket? I'll let you wear it for a week.

OBADIAH: He wants the tape.

JACK: No way! That's my Dad's tape. He'll kill me.

(Yellow shrugs his shoulder.)

JACK: Wait! Wait, okay. Yellow, you don't even have a VCR. You gotta have one of these boxes to make these tapes, run. It makes no sense to give you this, right?

(Yellow starts walking away.)

JACK: Wait, Yellow! Just wait and... Obie, what should I do?

OBADIAH: Give him the tape.

JACK: But... this isn't fair!

(Jack takes the tape out and puts it in a dust jacket. He hands it to Yellow.)

JACK: What are we gonna do?

OBADIAH: We?

JACK: Yeah! We're in this together, right?

(DOOR KNOCK. Obadiah thinks for a moment while Yellow exits and re-enters with Frenchy.)

JACK: Frenchy, what are you doing here? What is everyone doing here?!

FRENCHY: You know why I'm here.

JACK: No, I really don't. Do I have to pay her off too?!?

FRENCHY: You don't have to pay me nothing. I just came for what you owe me. Obie is taking care of things.

OBADIAH: I was going to get to it.

FRENCHY: Well then get to it.

OBADIAH: Jack, Frenchy thought it would be a good idea to have you take a step back from the fan club and the mural.

FRENCHY: We kicking you out.

JACK: You're kicking me out of an un-official fan club? For what?

FRENCHY: You been all up in our business, taking over shit. But you ain't taking over jack, Jack!

JACK: That's not true. My Dad was only trying to help your little project.

FRENCHY: We don't need his help.

JACK: Yeah, you do!

FRENCHY: We got our own help. The Black community can help itself.

JACK: You people are burning down your stores and homes! What do you mean you can help yourself? You've been here forever and you can't even put up a stupid mural of Michael Jackson.

OBADIAH: Jack, that's not fair.

JACK: It's not fair? What does fair have to do with it?!? Red stole from my mom's car last week. And I can't say anything because then everyone would turn against me. Is that fair?

FRENCHY: It was reparations.

JACK: Give me a break! Obie, are you listening to this stupid shit? This is why my dad says Blacks can't get ahead. You burn your own house down and then complain about the smoke. You steal and then want handouts.

OBADIAH: What do you mean by 'you?' I'm not stealing anything.

JACK: Oh, I didn't mean... you. You're different. You know that, right?

OBADIAH: No, Jack. I'm not different.

FRENCHY: Thank you, Obie.

JACK: You're not like her or Yellow.

FRENCHY: Divide and conquer. This is what the enemy does.

JACK: This is stupid! The 'enemy.' I'm not the enemy. I'm just a friend.

FRENCHY: The enemy always starts off as a friend. Even Hitler was a few people's friends before he got in charge.

OBADIAH: Okay, Frenchy. That's not cool. Jack is all right.

FRENCHY: Well I guess someone has had a change of heart. Guess Cracker Jack ain't getting kicked out. Is he, Obie?

OBADIAH: Frenchy, we just need to talk about it. We can work this out.

FRENCHY: I ain't working a damn thing out with Cracker Jack.

JACK: She's never been fair. Since the day I moved in, she's hated me. And I never did anything to her.

FRENCHY: You stole from me!

JACK: What did I steal?

(Frenchy looks at Obadiah.)

FRENCHY: You stole what I really cared about.

JACK: Your dumb fan club?

FRENCHY: Nah. It wasn't the club. It was what was in the fan club.

JACK: What is she talking about?

OBADIAH: I don't know.

FRENCHY: I guess Red was right about you, Obie.

SCENE FOUR

OBADIAH: *(holding paper)* When I first heard the news about Michael Jackson, I couldn't believe it. I mean, I drink Pepsi every day. Everyone was down for days. But I think we are all missing an important lesson. This is yet another reason why you shouldn't have a jheri curl. It's like pouring gasoline on your head. And it itches. I heard he went up like a roman candle. Burned away the top layer of his skin. They say your skin is the body's largest organ. What happens when you lose all of it that quickly? The doctors said it was just the top and they can patch him up with some plastic surgery. I feel bad for Michael. I hope he doesn't die. He should at least get a lifetime supply of Pepsi.

JACK: Why would you put something on your head that can catch on fire? It seems like pretty bad decision. I don't put anything on my hair. I just comb it in the morning and go. I hear that if you have this thing called a jheri curl you gotta spend hours every day in front of a mirror spraying juice on it. I asked Nasty Man what's in the juice and he said 'pretty little white boys who ask too many questions.' Well that was rude. And every time I ask someone at school they tease me. Why are people so sensitive about hair? It's just like fingernails to me. I don't know why Michael got rid of his Afro in the first place.

FRENCHY: I've written a letter to Michael Jackson every day he's been in the hospital. I figured maybe if I keep sending letters, one will get through. My mom says that he don't even read the letters. He has someone do it for him. But I know he'll read at least one. What else does he have to do but sit around in the hospital. In the last letter I included this: an afro pick. Get rid of the juice Michael and get back to your roots.

RED: I heard when he caught fire he just kept on dancing.

69

OBADIAH: Wow.

RED: Dancing through fire. And he didn't stop. They had to tackle him to the ground and pour water on him. Who knows? Maybe if nobody was looking he would've kept on dancing in the fire. I'd like to die like that: dancing in fire.

JACK: On the plus side, everyone has gotten excited about the mural again. A reporter from a paper even came out to talk to me. I was listed as the president of the Opa Locka Michael Jackson fan club. I know that must've made Frenchy upset but I don't care. It was cool to see my name in the paper.

OBADIAH: Jack was in the paper. Like the whole mural was his idea. I guess it's in print now. Can't do anything to change it. My parents were right. It really is all about the golden rule.

SCENE FIVE

(Obadiah is hanging out at Jack's place.)

OBADIAH: Jack, I've been thinking about something-

JACK: Obie: I have a surprise. I want to give you the eyes.

OBADIAH: What? I thought you were saving them for someone...special.

JACK: *(hands eyes to him)* I was.

OBADIAH: This is great. I can give these to Frenchy and then-

JACK: Obie, no...

(Jack snatches the eyes back. He starts to walk away and then calms down. He switches the conversation.)

JACK: Did you see the article in the paper?

OBADIAH: Yeah, I didn't know you had been elected president of the fan club.

JACK: Ha! Yeah the reporter made a mistake.

OBADIAH: My Mom said papers print corrections on mistakes they make.

JACK: Okay.

OBADIAH: If it was a mistake, can't you call and have them print a corrected copy.

JACK: I guess, but who cares? It's exciting to have the mural in the paper. My Dad said they can even throw a big party when it's time for it to be shown.

OBADIAH: Okay, Jack. But listen to me-

JACK: Oh, and don't worry about the tape. He was pissed off so I just told him Red stole it.

OBADIAH: Jack! You can't do that.

JACK: Hey, do you have a better idea? Obie this gets us outta trouble. And my Dad never liked Red and knows that he Yestole from us.

OBADIAH: What if he calls the police?

JACK: He's not. My Dad said he's given up and there's no point. Some people are beyond help.

OBADIAH: So all's well that ends well.

JACK: Yeah and he still likes you. And we can still play together. Even though you didn't stick up for me.

OBADIAH: What do you mean I didn't stick up for you?

JACK: Against Frenchy. You know she's always hated me but you still pretend like it's okay. But if I did that to her, you wouldn't be my friend.

OBADIAH: I've known her longer.

JACK: But I'm closer to you.

OBADIAH: No, you're not.

JACK: Yeah, I stick up for you. My mom didn't want me hanging out with you. When we first moved in and my Dad called you 'a name' I told him that you were different.

OBADIAH: What did your Dad call me?

JACK: I don't remember. But he was just angry and I stuck up for you. Even my mom gets quiet when he's like that. But I said something. And now he likes you. Have you ever done something like that for me?

OBADIAH: I appreciate it, Jack.

JACK: Then how come you make me feel bad about a silly title in a newspaper story. Why can't you be happy?

OBADIAH: Cause I messed up. But you can help me fix things.

JACK: How?

OBADIAH: The mural. Let me have the eyes. I can give them to Frenchy. Maybe then she won't be mad.

JACK: NO!

OBADIAH: Why not? I thought you said you were saving them for a special person.

JACK: Yeah, but not her.

OBADIAH: Says you?

JACK: Yeah, says me!

(OBADIAH looks at the eyes.)

OBADIAH: And what if I were to just take it?

JACK: But it's not your's. You'd be stealing.

OBADIAH: So what if did? After all, isn't that what you expect me to do? Isn't that the way I'm supposed to be.

JACK: You're not a thief.

OBADIAH: *(getting in his face)* Isn't that what your Dad thinks I am? Don't you think I am too? What are you gonna do, Cracker Jack. You're gonna fight me?

JACK: Obie, what are you doing?

OBADIAH: I'm stealing. That's what we do right? We steal and then ask for handouts! That's what you said!

JACK: But... I didn't mean it.

OBADIAH: I'm gonna give this to Frenchy. She's gonna be cool and everything is gonna return to normal.

(OBADIAH snatches the eyes from the mural and starts to leave.)

JACK: That's not true, Obie. I'm your friend.

OBADIAH: No you're not.

JACK: I AM! Look let's just have some fun. My dad has another tape.

OBADIAH: No more tapes, no more Nintendo, no more. You're not good for me. You're making me change and I don't like it.

JACK: I didn't make you change. You were like this all along.

OBADIAH: I was happier before you came. Things were simple. You guys stayed over there and the we lived over here. Red and Yellow, and Frenchy and we all were together.

JACK: OBIE, THEY'RE NOT LIKE YOU!

OBADIAH: Jack, some things you can't be a part of-

JACK: OBIE, THEY'RE JUST A STUPID, BUNCH OF WORTHLESS NIGGERS!!!

(BEAT)

OBADIAH: What?

JACK: They're not like you. You're different.

OBADIAH: If you tell your Dad about me taking the eyes, I'll tell everyone about the tapes and what your dad does to you. And then your family will have to move again.

(OBADIAH exits with the eyes.)

SCENE SIX

(Street corner outside Obadiah's home.)

FRENCHY: What do you mean we can't come over?

YELLOW: …his m-mother said we're n-not allowed.

FRENCHY: Not allowed? Why? It's been a week since he showed it. I need to see it.

YELLOW: H-heard C-Cracker Jack has a new tape play-er.

FRENCHY: It ain't the same thing. What's wrong with Obie? Leaving us out here. That ain't right.

YELLOW: …wuh…wuh…word.

FRENCHY: That's wrong. Yellow go ask him why?

YELLOW: Nuh…nuh…nah. I can't.

FRENCHY: Why not?

YELLOW: I…g-got his s-sister's bike.

FRENCHY: Forget them. Tired of going over to they stu-pid house anyway. Think they all that just because they got a VCR. When Frenchy Carter grows up, Imma get ten VCRs. Big fat ones, like Zenith.

YELLOW: …yeah…

FRENCHY: And they ain't gonna say shit. Have my own private screenings. My own special shows… my own family.

YELLOW: …yuh…yuh.. yo, I h-heard dat.

76

FRENCHY: Ewwww. Why you talking like that?

YELLOW: G-got a t-tape by R-Run D…M…C…

FRENCHY: Sounds stupid.

(BEAT)

FRENCHY: Let me borrow it from you?
(Yellow shakes his head)
Why not? You probably stole it.

YELLOW: D-did not.

FRENCHY: You and your brother are going to burn in hell. Bunch of retarded-ass felons.

YELLOW: Fuh…fuh…fuck you…Frenchy.

FRENCHY: High-yellow retarded ass. Think you special cause you light skinned?

YELLOW: Yup.

FRENCHY: Fuck you then. I'm Black and beautiful. Just like Michael Jackson. When I grow up I'm going to be his queen. Then I won't have to go over to Obie's house. Fuck this, I'm gonna get a errenge soda and some pop rocks.

(Frenchy exits. Yellow follows after her.)

YELLOW: C-careful! Duh..don't m-mix them together. F -Frenchy? C-can I ha-ve a sip?

SCENE SEVEN

(Frenchy walks by Obadiah on her way to the store. She sucks her teeth and keeps moving.)

OBADIAH: Frenchy?

FRENCHY: ...yeah?

OBADIAH: We're having a memorial service of "Thriller" at my house. Maybe raise some money for Michael and his skin that got burned off. We've raised 75 cents and three watermelon Now and Laters. Wanna show up?

FRENCHY: Nah... I don't need to see it. Cracker Jack can take my place.

OBADIAH: Why are you acting stank?

FRENCHY: Don't tell me about acting stank. Your whole style is stank. Thinking you're so big and bad just because you're the only one with a VCR.

OBADIAH: I do not.

FRENCHY: Then why are you going to shut us out?

OBADIAH: I had to.

FRENCHY: Why?

OBADIAH: I... I was busy.

FRENCHY: You busy a lot.

OBADIAH: And what if I am? Is that a problem?

FRENCHY: Nah, I guess you can do whatever.

OBADIAH: Damn, Frenchy. Why are you making this so difficult?

FRENCHY: I'm being difficult? Fine, then let me make it easy for you. Seeya later!

OBADIAH: I got something for you.

FRENCHY: Keep it.

OBADIAH: Frenchy this is big. This is what you really wanted.

FRENCHY: Obie, you don't even know what I really want.

OBADIAH: It's about the mural.

FRENCHY: Oh, you mean the mural created by your friend Cracker Jack, president of the MJ fan club?

OBADIAH: Yeah. And he said he was sorry about the article. The reporter got his title wrong.

FRENCHY: Whatever. I don't care anymore.

OBADIAH: I was going to give you this from the mural.

FRENCHY: Obie, fuck the mural! Damn! It's ruined anyway. Cracker Jack and his Dad, you, and this whole city ruined my-

OBADIAH: -stop blaming him, okay? You blame me, you blame Red, you blame Cracker Jack. You're always blaming people. You love to be pretend like you had nothing to do with it.

FRENCHY: Oh, you telling me about myself like you're the HNIC.

OBADIAH: Maybe I am.

FRENCHY: Setting all these rules like you the head nigga in charge. I'm the HNIC. And I'm quitting this. Goodbye, Obie. Don't call, don't stop by, when you see me in school don't say hi cause I won't be saying shit back to you.

OBADIAH: Frenchy... this is the last time sharing this. You're gonna miss out. We won't be a family anymore.

FRENCHY: A family? Where did you get that from?

OBADIAH: *(exiting)* Nevermind.

FRENCHY: Go get Cracker Jack to look at it with you. You and your cracker friend licking each other...

OBADIAH: What?

FRENCHY: ...like he's vanilla and you're chocolate ice cream.

OBADIAH: Shut the fuck up, Frenchy.

FRENCHY: Yellow told me you were trying to lick Jack. Trying to lick the white right off him.

OBADIAH: He didn't.

FRENCHY: He did. He said youze a faggot. Figured that. Well I don't need any yellow faggots in my life.

(BEAT)

OBADIAH: Forget you. I can hate you too. Buck tooth, snaggle tooth, charcoal nigger bitch. You think anyone will ever love your ugly midnight ass? You wish you looked like me, you project monkey. *(he laughs)* And you talk about Michael Jackson marrying you? Only if the fire burned his eyes out and his nose away so he wouldn't have to see your chimp-ugly face and smell your funky daisy dukes. Michael Jackson ain't never going to marry you because all you is, is some dark ghetto trash nigger bitch.

SCENE EIGHT

(CITY COMMISSIONER presents plaque to Jack in front of the mural. They laugh and grin.)

CITY COMMISSIONER: As your city commissioner, I welcome you to this wonderful event. We are so happy to be here today to honor a national treasure: Michael Jackson. And the city of Opa Locka has taken special efforts to make sure Mr. Jackson's image lasts forever with this beautiful new mural completed thanks to the efforts of our own sons and daughters. And especially due to the dedication of Ron and his son, Wes, who is – as I understand it- president of the Opa Locka Michael Jackson fan club. You must be pretty proud of yourself, young man.

JACK: Um... thanks.

CITY COMMISSIONER: How does it feel to have this finally complete?

JACK: Good.

CITY COMMISSIONER: So you're happy?

JACK: Yeah.

CITY COMMISSIONER: *(aside to Jack)* Look, kid give me a break here.

JACK: A break of what?

CITY COMMISSIONER: Just say something. We got local news here taping. (back to crowd) So any words for us today?

JACK: My Dad said he believes the mural might give people hope.

CITY COMMISSIONER: Yes, yes indeed son. We could all use a little hope.

JACK: My Dad said that the reason why people like Michael Jackson is because he's a real American. And because he worked hard nobody sees him as just Black. They see him as an American who keeps getting better every year. And if you... I mean if we just stopped complaining and worked harder we would be just like Michael Jackson. And there would be less complaining and asking for handouts in the...in the community.

CITY COMMISSIONER: Well! That is a very... interesting statement. And I'm sure we are all going to digest that thoroughly, Wes. I know I am.

JACK: My Dad said people in this neighborhood should smile more. And not look so angry. Because when you look angry no one wants to give you a job and then you're stuck-

CITY COMMISSIONER: -a big hand for Wes, everyone. Yes, kids say the darndest things, don't they?

JACK: Actually my Dad said that.

CITY COMMISSIONER: Well the apple doesn't fall far from the tree. Yes, Blacks are certainly familiar with the "Strange Fruit" that falls from the American tree. And your Dad's words just helped remind us of that. Let's clap it up for Wes and the Opa Locka fan club. In fact let's have some of your co-partners up here. I understand there were some others who helped you out. Do you wanna invite them up on stage with you?

(Jack shrugs his shoulders.)

CITY COMMISSIONER: Let's get at least one other helper up here. A young man named Obie was your assistant. Come on up, young man.

(Obadiah reluctantly walks up on stage and stands on the other side of the City Commissioner.)

CITY COMMISSIONER: There he is. Such a fine look-ing young man. And we have some local businesses I also want to thank for sponsoring-

(FRENCHY marches up on the stage.)

CITY COMMISSIONER: Yes, young lady is there a problem?

FRENCHY: Well... *(losing a bit of nerve)* ...well... I wanted... well... well...

CITY COMMISSIONER: Yes, well well well. There will be time for individual pictures with the mural after the ceremony. So you can just go and sit down. Right now.

FRENCHY: But I'm in the club. I'm the president.

CITY COMMISSIONER: *(laughs)* Well I believe Jack is the president.

JACK: Actually...

FRENCHY: I am. And... well I want to stand on this stage. Because this is my project. This is my mural, this is my town, this is my Michael.

CITY COMMISSIONER: 'My Michael.' Isn't she just precious? *(aside to her)* Look, you lil' raggedy nappy-headed fool: you better sit your ass back down with your Mama and quit fucking wit' my hustle! *(back to audience)* Kids say the darndest things, don't they? Now let's get you off the stage, lil girl-

OBADIAH: -Let her stay. She helped out.

CITY COMMISSIONER: Oh. Okay, All right, Miss Well Well Well. I guess you can stay up here. Lord knows you could use some manners but you can't help how you was raised. Just take a few steps back. Now take a few more. Good. Okay, don't get in the first picture. Or the second or third. That's reserved for the big boys, right fellas?

(City Commissioner grabs Obadiah and Jack as cameras flash. Frenchy watches all her glory, dreams, and efforts go to others.

Lights shift to Frenchy.)

FRENCHY: It was a sloppy job. My grandma makes ceramics down at the community center and she said the mural didn't look right. The artist they hired was a friend of Ron's and never had any experience doing ceramic murals. He didn't burn the tiles in the fire at the right temperature. And when it rained a week later all the color dripped off. But the check had cleared and the artist was gone. We were left with this ghost-white MJ. Some people said it looked more like Andrew Jackson than Michael. Everyone pitched in and repainted it. Then when it rained again and the paint ran away from Michael, a smaller group of people got together the following weekend and painted it. But after a few months people just got tired of repainting the mural. When the next riots hit, some rocks swiped the top of the mural and parts of Michael's forehead disappeared. Then a hurricane took off his chin. And pieces of the hair chipped away. Some taggers started putting their gang logos in the gaps, promoters were pasting little stickers for upcoming shows on him and pretty soon Michael's face was something else. Ads, Bugs Bunny, malt liquor, lucky numbers, and dirty jokes. The only thing left were the eyes.

(BEAT)

FRENCHY: And so one day when it was Christmas in August and the streets were hot with tear gas and smoke, I went down to the mural. I stood in front of these pair of eyes. And I remembered how things used to be on this block. My old friends and all those songs we used to listen to back in the day. I remembered all this.

(BEAT)

FRENCHY: And I smashed each eye until they were empty little holes. Next week those holes were filled with promos for the new summer movies. No one even noticed.

SCENE NINE

OBADIAH: 1984 disintegrated in little pieces before my eyes. Like bits of sky or sun burnt skin. Bit by bit it all fell down. The neighborhood changed. Latinos and Whites moved in, raising the property values, which meant black families were forced to move out. Fast food, grocery stores and delis arrived. And so did crack and AIDS. Friends and neighbors we had known for years started dying. Their mouths would shrivel up and their eyes would bulge out of their heads and a desperate panting would come across their face as if they were saying 'save me.' But we could only watch. My cousin Francine started using heroin and became one of the first women in America to die from AIDS. The doctors panicked and didn't know what to do with her. They said her body just quit. The autopsy said it was pneumonia. VCRs went on sale that summer and became the hot Christmas item that year. Along with the Apple, if you could afford the luxury of a personal computer. Run DMC's record became the first rap album to go gold and the beginning of a new attitude in America.

(BEAT)

OBADIAH: Red became a professional criminal, known for pistol whipping and knifing his victims. He was the meanest man in town until the police shot him dead for trying to rob a McDonald's. Shortly afterward, his brother, Yellow, just disappeared one day. Frenchy got pregnant. And then got pregnant again. And then got pregnant for the third time before she was 18. Years of living amongst us turned Jack into a Republican political consultant who believed in trickle-down Reaganomics and the end of affirmative action. I think he's still angry at us. Maybe we should have learned his name. Maybe he should have learned ours. I discovered what that strange feeling was and buried it like a ticking bomb. Then there's Michael Jackson. He recovered from the fire, but he wasn't the same. Maybe it was the trauma of almost being burned to death, maybe it was the money, or maybe it was because the world was crumbling so fast. He became suspicious of everything. Overly-protective and even more shy and quiet. The changes were slow and each time we saw our hero, we recognized him a little bit less. It looked like he was dying.

(LIGHTS SHIFT. Obadiah looks at mural.)

OBADIAH: Some of my friends said he was on crack. Others said he looked so skinny and pale because he got AIDS. But the truth was a lot more painful. He was the one who was killing himself, piece by piece. It sounds silly but to a child living in Opa Locka, it felt like he was trying to kill me too. Bit by bit he was poisoning us. And so we killed him first. In our tape decks, in our minds, on our radio stations we killed him. We let him fade from our memories so that it was easier to laugh at him. Make jokes about this strange man with a high-pitched voice. This grotesque, pale Tiny Tim with a button nose and razor-thin lips. And then one bright calm day, I sat down to have lunch when I got the news. Michael Jackson. Dead.

(BEAT)

OBADIAH: My God... I haven't even thought about him in...

(Obadiah tries to eat, but can't.)

OBADIAH: I walked out of the restaurant and down the street. It was such a nice day. People were dining outside in sidewalk cafes whispering 'well you know Michael' and 'it is so sad.' Businessmen were staring at the iPhone screens in the middle of the crosswalk. And I fought the overwhelming urge to run. Why did I care so much? Who cares? Millions of people die every year. And where the hell was I walking to? My feet carried my body as my thoughts drifted. I haven't listened to a Michael Jackson album in... wow...

(Lights shift to Yvonne "Frenchy" Clark's House. Clarence, aka YELLOW, is putting on his jacket. He speaks slow and soft to avoid stuttering too much. They are grown and married.)

FRENCHY: You're leaving now?

YELLOW: I want to go down to the hall.

FRENCHY: Why?

YELLOW: For the mural. P-people will be gathering there.

FRENCHY: Clarence, no one in this town even remembers that dumb mural.

YELLOW: We do.

FRENCHY: It doesn't matter. There's nothing left of it.

YELLOW: How do you know?

FRENCHY: I just do.

YELLOW: We'll see about that.

FRENCHY: What do you mean 'we?'

YELLOW: You're coming.

FRENCHY: Clarence, I have to clean up around here. Make sure that Ernest does his homework. I just can't go down-

YELLOW: -Baby, we're saying goodbye to Michael. Can't you spare a minute?

(BEAT)

FRENCHY: Wait for me. I just got to fix myself up.

YELLOW: No, baby. You're beautiful natural.

FRENCHY: You're just saying that so I won't take forever to get ready.

YELLOW: Yup. But also cause it's true. You're my chocolate chip.

FRENCHY: Okay but let me do my hair and put on some makeup.

YELLOW: No, baby. Come as you are. Just as you are.

(They exit.)

SCENE TEN

(Setting: Opa Locka City Hall. Mural. Jack stands there holding a flashlight into the space where the mural should be. Frenchy and Yellow enter.)

JACK: This was it.

FRENCHY: Excuse me, sir…

JACK: It was right here. The mural was on this building.

FRENCHY: I didn't think anyone would be down here.

JACK: There were a few other people who stopped by. But that's been about it. I can't believe it. I haven't thought about Michael Jackson in…

FRENCHY: Years.

YELLOW: Decades.

JACK: 1984. That's when we did this.

YELLOW: We?

JACK: Yes, I lived around the block. I'm Wes.

YELLOW: Wes. Wes? Wait…are you...

JACK: Cracker Jack.

YELLOW: Honey this is Cracker Jack…I mean, Jack. Well, I mean...

FRENCHY: Oh, cool. Been a while. You still live here?

JACK: O God no! I mean, no. My family, we moved a long time ago to… to another part of town where…

YELLOW: Totally understand.

JACK: Yeah, back then it was just, ah, it was just really...

FRENCHY: Agreed...it was just really...something.

JACK: And you're Frenchy?

FRENCHY: Yvonne. *(pointing to spot on mural)*

YELLOW: Clarence. *(Jack looks confused)* Yellow.

JACK: You're right. The mural was on this building.

JACK: Oh. I can't tell where though.

FRENCHY: Here it is. Right here. You can still see the outline of...

(Frenchy gets a bit emotion.)

JACK: Is something wrong?

YELLOW: No, nothing. She was just a b-big fan...

JACK: So was I, but I guess you win the competition of who was the biggest Michael Jackson fan in Opa Locka.

FRENCHY: What?

JACK: He is yours again.

FRENCHY: Yeah, he's ours again. Now that he's dead, we get to have him back.

YELLOW: Honey.

OBADIAH: *(entering)* Wow, there's actually people down here.

FRENCHY: Obie?

OBADIAH: Yvonne! *(they hug)* Yellow?

YELLOW: Clarence. I left Yellow behind a long time ago.

OBADIAH: Of course. What happened to our mural?

FRENCHY: I destroyed it.

YELLOW: Honey, what are you talking about?

JACK: From what I remember the mural deteriorated and the city just didn't keep good maintenance on it. And there were all those riots and graffiti artists.

OBADIAH: Wes?

JACK: Hi, Obie. Looking good. How are things going?

OBADIAH: I was eating lunch when I found out and I just spaced. I've just been walking around the past few hours.

(Obadiah goes up to the mural. Frenchy follows him and they share a moment. Jack and Yellow go off to the side and talk quietly.)

FRENCHY: Obie, the eyes were right there. They reminded me of your eyes. See.

OBADIAH: Yvon, you didn't really destroy it?

FRENCHY: His eyes were like black pearls.

(BEAT)

JACK: Well... this is great catching up with you guys. We should all hang out some time?

OBADIAH: Ummm... sure, I guess we could all...

FRENCHY: Stop being phony.

YELLOW: Yvon.

FRENCHY: You know we won't ever do that. After that year we all hated each other. But I am glad to see you all tonight. Even you Wes.

JACK: Thanks.

FRENCHY: So as the president of the Opa Locka Michael Jackson fan club let's just say a few words and leave. That year is gone and so is... *(sighs and points at the empty space where the mural was)* I'll start. *(to mural)* Michael: I love you, baby. You were our Black prince. Beautiful, graceful, magical. And now you're gone. I will always love you. Goodbye my beautiful prince.

YELLOW: Michael. You were brother and my heart. I wouldn't have made it through my childhood without your voice. And every time I hear your music, I think of my brother, Ernest. Most people knew him as...as 'Red.' He was h-half of me. You were the other half. Now you're both gone. So I guess that 'me' is gone forever. Goodbye brother.

JACK: Michael: there will never be another. I always wanted to dance like you, sing like you. You were so powerful and gentle. And even though I'm an old white dude... you made me feel like I was in your family. And you made me apart of this family right here. Goodbye Michael.

OBADIAH: Michael. Brother. I am so sorry but I have to say this: I hated you for a long time. For a long, long time. You hurt me so bad. You betrayed me. But... I hated only as much as I first loved. And I thought you betrayed my family only because I betrayed them first. So I want to apologize to everyone here and to you. I don't have any more hatred in my heart and I don't have any more nostalgia for the good ol' days of 1984. That was a long time ago. You can rest now. I love you brother.

FRENCHY: I guess this is the last meeting of the Michael Jackson fan club. Obie, do you have a closing treasury report?

OBADIAH: I think I still have a few watermelon Now and Laters. But the treasury closes with its initial seed grant of $1. Paid for and returned to the president.

(OBADIAH hands her $1.)

FRENCHY: If that's the last financial report then this meeting is adjourned. I dissolve this organization, our constitution, and our ties. Goodbye...family.

OBADIAH: We lost our Michael. The hero we first saw ourselves in. And the one we first erased. Our tormentor and our gentle prince. The prodigal son who left us and the one who came back home. Our brother. And that time, that neighborhood, and that piece of our childhood: it all crumbled. Like pieces of the sky. Disintegrating into air and light. A memory.

(The neighborhood slowly fades away into darkness and oblivion.)

THE END

NOTES

NOTES

NOTES

NOTES

Made in the USA
Columbia, SC
28 July 2022